DRUGS, TEENS, AND RECOVERY

Real-life Stories of Trying to Stay Clean

DRUGS, TEENS, AND RECOVERY

Real-life Stories of Trying to Stay Clean

Glenn Alan Cheney

—Issues in Focus—

ENSLOW PUBLISHERS, INC.

Bloy St. & Ramsey Ave.	P.O. Box 38
Box 777	Aldershot
Hillside, N.J. 07205	Hants GU12 6BP
U.S.A.	U.K.

Library of Congress Cataloging-in-Publication Data

Cheney, Glenn Alan.
     Drugs, teens, and recovery : real-life stories of trying to stay
clean / Glenn Alan Cheney
          p.   cm. — (Issues in focus)
     Includes bibliographical references and index.
     ISBN 0-89490-431-0
     1. Teenagers—United States—Drug use. 2. Recovering addicts
United States. I. Title. II. Series: Issues in focus (Hillside,
N.J.
HV5824.Y68C48 1993
362.29'0835—dc20   92-39722
                                                         CIP

Printed in the United States of America

10 9 8 7 6 5 4 3 2

Illustration credits: Glenn Alan Cheney

Cover Illustration: Glenn Alan Cheney

Contents

Introduction

This book tells the stories of seven teens and drugs. The youngest started getting involved with drugs at the age of seven. The oldest was a mother by her eighteenth birthday. The wide variety of situations presented here is intended to show that drug use is not simply an inner-city problem. Most of the teens profiled are in recovery, and if they're lucky, they'll be recovering for the rest of their lives. Statistically, however, many of them are likely to start using again. Some still deny that they have a problem. Some of those in recovery went down pretty far before they bottomed out. None of them died, but some of their friends did.

This book focuses on drug users who have taken the first step along the road to recovery. Unfortunately, they represent a minority of users. Most keep using well into adulthood. They hold jobs, but normally not very good ones, and often not for long. They raise families, but their marriages are usually miserable and often end in divorce or abandonment. Their children tend to be unhappy as they see their parents care more about drugs than their children. Very often, the addicted parents pave the way for their children's use. Also, drug users tend to die at a younger age, sometimes due to poor health, sometimes as victims of violence, and very often because of drug-related accidents.

The real stories presented here were told by the young people themselves. Their names have been changed and the people you see in the photos are models who have agreed to have their picture shown, not the actual people who told their stories. But, we must acknowledge the courage of the addicts who speak out about their addictions. The tone of their words reflects their thoughts and feelings. None of them is proud of using drugs; all of them are sorry they ever started. Those who have started the recovery process are deeply thankful that they've been able to go clean, for a while at least. They all know that they will never be free from the urge to use. Though years into recovery, their particular addictions still whisper to them, tempting them to try it just one more time . . . just once.

1

Bobby

With his blond hair and blue eyes, Bobby could be a model or an actor in a soap opera. When he was in high school, he earned extra money playing guitar in a band and working as a clerk in a supermarket. He comes from an upper middle-class family in an affluent California town of about 40,000 people. It's a town that puts a lot of money into its school system because it wants its kids to become successful adults. But the kids don't always turn out that way. Bobby was twenty years old when he felt secure enough to reflect back on his experience as a high school student. Here he tells the story of his teenage years that were, in his words, a complete waste.

"When I was in elementary school, I was cool. I was always the center of attention. Everybody wanted to be with me. But when I went to junior high, that changed. The school had kids from half a dozen other elementary schools. All of a sudden I wasn't the most popular kid around. A lot of my friends found other friends. I ended up with a bunch of kids I didn't really like. They were kind of stuck up. They thought they were cool, and that meant it was cool to be with them. I wanted to be cool, so there I was.

"Meanwhile, my parents were getting a divorce. I can't blame them for everything that happened to me, but I guess the divorce had something to do with it. I was pretty mad about it. And as I got worse with the drugs and alcohol, my relationship with them got worse. And the worse it got with them, the more I needed someone else to accept me. I needed those friends who weren't really friends. And I thought I needed the drugs to make me feel good.

"I was thirteen when I first smoked pot. I was hanging with another kid when an older kid, a senior in high school, offered us a joint. We smoked it and felt very cool. I don't know if we really got high or were just pretending, just showing off for each other. We ran around the house acting crazy. Then we went in to make brownies. We ended up laughing ourselves silly and eating the dough.

"By my freshman year in high school, I was smoking all day long. I'd smoke first thing in the morning and find a chance to smoke three or four times during school. We'd go anywhere we could to grab a couple of hits—up on the roof, out in a corner of the playground, under the bleachers at the football field. Sometimes I'd walk home to a secret place I had in a thicket of bamboo.

"I don't know how I got away with it. I wore sunglasses all the time and fell asleep in class a lot. I never studied. Not once. The funny thing is, I never flunked a course. I got real good at sweet-talking teachers. They liked me. They let me slide by with C's and D's. I'm sure they knew I was stoned, but they never said anything. I don't know why not. Once another kid and I were smoking under some steps that led up to the gym. The coach suddenly came out of the gym and down the steps. He smelled the smoke and looked under the steps. He said, 'Bobby, is that you?' and peeked down between the steps.

"I said 'Yep,' trying to hold smoke in my lungs.

"'What are you doing under there?'

"'Nothing,' I said.

"And all he said was, 'Oh, all right.' Then he walked away. I'm sure he must have smelled the smoke.

"I don't know why, but I never got caught, never got lectured to, never got warned to use drugs except in posters and on TV. Nobody ever told me to try harder in school. I got away with everything, a lot of it pretty bad stuff.

"I was about fifteen when I went home with a kid who wasn't really a friend, just somebody I knew. There

11

was a bottle of gin in his parents' liquor cabinet. I started drinking shots and washing them down with orange juice. I think I drank eight or ten shots. Then we went out. I don't remember much of what happened. I was throwing up all over the place. We ended up down in a part of town where drunks hang out. I got into some kind of fight with somebody twice my size. Somehow the kid with me talked the other guy out of killing me. Then he put me on a bus and asked the driver to throw me off at the corner near my house. I guess he did. I have no idea how I ended up at home.

"I stole a lot. My parents never gave me money, and I never wanted it from them. Other kids could ask their parents for twenty or thirty dollars any time. But I wanted to be free and independent. I had a job in a supermarket, just to prove my independence. But for drug money, I stole. I didn't take much from my own parents, but when I'd sleep over at another kid's house, I'd get into his parents' bedroom and see what I could take.

"I can't express the torment I was feeling during those first couple of years in high school. I was always totally tensed up, partly from fear of getting caught, partly from fear of being rejected by kids I thought were cool, partly from fear of flunking. I'd have an ounce of grass in my pocket, a pint of vodka in a milk carton, and a big wad of cash that wasn't mine. I always had a million lies to juggle in my head, lies to teachers, other kids, and my parents. I always walked with my head down so people wouldn't know I was stoned. Until today, my posture's bad from walking around hunched over and all tensed up.

"In the summer after my sophomore year, I got in with a bunch of older kids, some of them in college. I though that was great. Now I was *real* cool. I dropped my other friends, who I hated, and hung out with these older kids, who really accepted me. They turned me on to acid and cocaine. Coke was totally cool, and acid was great. For three bucks I could stay high for ten hours. I tripped every weekend for the whole summer and was stoned or drunk all the rest of the time.

"Our big thing was to get totally bonkers. We'd mix grain alcohol with Kool-Aid and smoke cigarettes laced with coke, and of course joints. Then we'd go find some public place and trash it until the cops came. It was a big sport, getting chased by the cops. They never caught us, at least not me, and I never got in trouble.

"Once we burned down an abandoned building. The cops didn't know who did it until my mother overheard me talking about it on the phone. She turned us in. We were supposed to do a bunch of hours of community service down at the fire station, but they never called us and we never did it.

"It was important to me not to spend my own money on drugs. Either I'd steal money for it or I'd buy a big quantity and sell enough of it to pay for it all. Then I'd use the rest. I had a good relationship with my dealer, who was a senior in the same high school. He'd trust me with dope to sell, or he'd let me pay in a couple of weeks.

"Once another kid and I were searching through his parents' closet because we knew they used drugs. They had a safe. I pulled on the handle, and it opened. Inside was a big stock of hundred dollar bills. We pulled a bunch out of the middle and ran. It was $2,000. We got a big disk of hash and a lot of coke. We were all set for the next month and a half. And we never got caught, either. All I can figure is that it was illegal money, and the kid's father couldn't report it to the police.

"In less than two years I wrecked three or four cars, but I never got in trouble for it. I never drove drunk—somehow I knew *that* was bad—but every accident was drug related. Either I was stoned, or going to get drugs, or pay for them, or look around for some. Three days after I got my license, I was doing about seventy in my father's BMW while trying to light a pipe. I rear-ended a Mercedes Benz. Somehow I managed to talk my way out of it, and I got away. Of course my parents knew when I'd had an accident, but they never kept me from driving.

"After the divorce, I was living with my mother. Every once in a while when I wasn't stoned, we'd have a good time together. We'd make popcorn and watch TV and laugh and talk. I really liked it. But when I was high, I was always uptight and just short of violence. Anything would touch me off. I couldn't talk with anybody in my

14

family without starting to shout and scream. Sometimes I'd be tripping right in front of them. They must have known, but they never said anything. Once my mother stopped at the post office and asked me to put two letters in the 'Local' mailbox. I stood there for a long trying to figure out which of the two boxes to use. Finally I had to go ask her. Then I went back and tried again but still couldn't do it. I was totally confused even though there was nothing to be confused about.

"It was in my junior year when it got really bad. One morning I overslept, and my mother wouldn't give me a note for school. I screamed and swore at her, and before I left, I kicked a hole in the wall. Later I felt bad about it and was going to apologize, but when I got home, the phone was ringing. I answered. It was the school principal calling for my mother. I listened on the downstairs phone while they talked. I'll never forget her words. She said, 'I want him out of my life. I want him out of my house. I don't care if you sent him to Timbuktu.'

"I was shocked beyond belief. The one person in the world a kid could always count on was throwing me out. I ran upstairs, mad as hell, and shouted at her. She had a day care business going at the time, and I ended up yelling at all the little kids, trying to make them cry. She kept telling me to get out, so I grabbed some clothes, stuffed some cash into my wallet, and called a friend to pick me up. I stayed with him four or five days and then went to live with my father, who still lived in the same town.

"I never liked my father. Now he tried to make me happy. He let me do whatever I wanted. He gave me a curfew but didn't bother to enforce it. He let me buy a car, which I wrecked in no time at all. When he went on business trips, I threw huge parties in the house.

"Once another kid and I were smoking reefer in my bedroom. Suddenly Dad walked in and accused us of doing exactly what we were doing. But I got real mad at him and screamed and started pushing him. I had a fist up and was ready to slug him. My friend went out to his car to wait. My father said, 'Tell me to my face you weren't smoking dope.'

"I did it. As usual, I did a superb job of lying. He believed me. Then he asked if I wanted him to apologize to my friend. I said yes, and he actually did it. I feel terrible about doing that to him, but at the time, I thought it was funny. I laughed at him.

"It was in the last couple of weeks of my junior year when I ran into a couple of friends who had just gotten back from a rehab place. They were straight. They told me how intense the rehab place was. It had bowling lanes, an indoor swimming pool, everything. Best of all, any kid who went there, they said, automatically got straight A's for that semester. I had final exams coming up the next week, and I knew I was going to flunk them all. If going into rehab could get me out of that, I was all

16

for it. Not that I had any thoughts of going straight. I just figured I'd have a little vacation and get easy A's.

"Then they asked me if I ever felt like going to an AA meeting. Alcoholics Anonymous. They were going that night. They said that if I went, it'd be easier to get into rehab. I thought, hey, why not. I sped off to my mother's house to tell her. On the way, I wrecked the car against a stone wall. It barely hobbled to her driveway. I said I was going to an AA meeting. She said, 'Fine,' and didn't say anything about the car.

"I got all smoked up right before the meeting, kind of joking with myself that it was the last time in my life. I had no intention of taking the meeting seriously.

"Then, I walked into the meeting and was instantly accepted by everybody. They threw their arms around my shoulders. They wanted to hear what I had to say. They understood. They'd been there. For the first time in years, people were accepting me for who I was, even though I was stoned. And I was afraid that if I kept drinking and doing dope, I'd wind up being rejected again. It didn't make any difference to people in the meeting whether you were using alcohol or drugs. They were both bad, both basically the same thing, and you had to stop it all if you wanted your life to be good again. At the first meeting, I knew I was going to do whatever it took to stay clean.

"I still wake up thinking about getting high. I think about what I'm supposed to do for the AA meeting and just am not able to face all the hard work. But, for now, AA gives me someplace to go where I know everyone understands me.

"It's hard work trying to be totally honest with myself and with everyone else. There's no lies to juggle. It's weird, but I got so used to lying, cheating, and stealing that somehow not doing those things feels strange."

Questions about Alcohol

What happens when you drink alcohol?

When alcohol is swallowed, it is diluted by the stomach juices and is very quickly distributed throughout the body. The absorbed alcohol is passed through the liver. Then, it enters the bloodstream and is eventually converted into carbon dioxide and water. Alcohol's effect on the mind depends in large part on how quickly the alcohol is consumed and how much of it is consumed.

Which is less likely to get you drunk— beer, wine, or hard liquor?

The body can handle a third of an ounce of pure alcohol (or three-quarters of an ounce of 80-proof liquor) per hour. It doesn't matter what kind of drink that alcohol is in. A bottle of beer, a shot of hard liquor, and a glass of wine all have roughly equal amounts of alcohol. The quantities of any given alcoholic beverage that one can drink without getting drunk will vary from person to person, depending on weight and overall tolerance, but the ultimate effect is the same.

Is alcohol a drug?

Yes, alcohol is a drug that alters the way in which the body and mind function. With increasing amounts of alcohol, judgment is impaired, and reactions slow down. Eventually, liver cells may die and brain cells may be damaged. Alcohol also produces several other symptoms in the body.

How do you know if you're an alcoholic?

Alcoholics are often the last to recognize their problem. They often make a conscious effort to deny it. An alcoholic is someone who has a history of problem drinking. The problems may be in social, work, school, or health-related areas. If your problems can be associated with or made worse by alcohol use, then there is a problem. If the answer to the majority of the following questions is yes, you may have an alcohol problem.

A. Has anyone recommended that you cut back or stop drinking?

B. Have you ever felt annoyed or angry if anyone commented on your drinking?

C. Have there been times when you felt guilty about or regretted things that happened because of your drinking?

D. Have you ever used alcohol to help you get started in the morning or to steady your nerves?

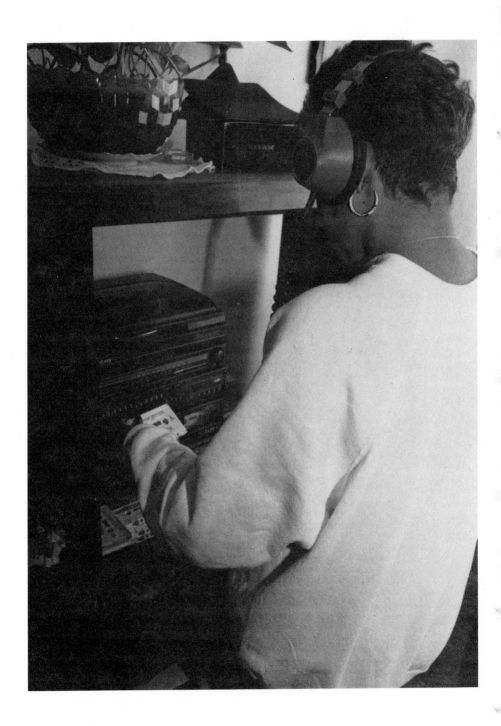

2

Prudencia

Prudencia lives in a medium-sized industrial town in southern Texas. Her Hispanic blood is obvious in her black hair and dark eyes. She's a bit on the short side but graced with the emerging figure of a young woman. Her temper tends to be friendly until it boils over. She likes to hang out with friends, maybe talking in the park, maybe shooting pool in a social club. She used to wear a lot of gold and fancy clothes, but these days she likes to keep it simple. It's safer.

"I started smoking weed when I was seven. I stole a couple of joints from my father when he came to visit my mother. It was very cool to be smoking on the way to school and then after school. To tell you the truth, I think it helped me in school. It slowed me down and made it seem like everything was happening real slow.

And I was like really *into* whatever the teacher was talking about. I'd pay attention like it was a magic show or something. If I wasn't stoned, I'd be making trouble with other kids and going to the bathroom all the time just to get up and do something. Nobody ever told me to stop or that it was wrong. To me, it was just normal.

"At the time I was living with my mother only. My father had moved out when I was four but was always coming back for some reason. My mom and I hated each other. We used to scream and fight all the time, call each other terrible names.

"When I was twelve, my boyfriend introduced me to coke. I loved it. I was hooked immediately. To get money for it, I stole from my mother. She had her own business delivering products to people and collecting the money. There was always a lot of cash at home, in a special money bag with a lock on it. But I knew where the key was so I used to just grab a handful of money any time I needed to buy, which was every day. Once I took $400 or $500 and spent it all on coke for my boyfriend and also my friend Madeline. My mother didn't watch the money too carefully; that's how I got away with it.

"I did coke constantly. I'd do it in school, just lay out a line on a book, then pretend to be sleepy and put my head down and sniff it up. I'd sniff up big long lines, more than most people would do all day.

"I stole a lot. I'd steal cars, steal stuff from stores,

24

break into houses, whatever I had to do to get money for drugs.

"Know how dumb I was about drugs? I stopped going to school. My boyfriend, Joe, and I were basically living together. I loved him so much. He really made me grow up. I was cooking for him, cleaning up after him, bathing him. It didn't matter what he did. When you love someone, you love them no matter what—or at least I did.

"He came home drunk all the time and would beat me. I always had a black eye or something. He was always telling me it was my fault, that he had to beat me up because I was fooling around or didn't respect him or something, which of course wasn't true because I loved him so much. And meanwhile *he* was fooling around with an older woman who had *kids*. It was like I was the wife and she was the girlfriend. She bought him a car and used to bail him out of jail all the time. He'd be in for stolen cars, driving without a license, always something to do with cars. I thought there was nothing I could do about the way he treated me. I was living in hell and didn't know it. I thought it was normal.

"I decided to stop using coke one day when I was thirteen. I had about $500 on me and was looking all over for some stuff, but nobody had any. So instead, I decided to go to the mall and just spend the whole five hundred. And I did. I bought sneakers, a jacket, anything I wanted. It was the first time in my life I really bought stuff I could own. I loved it! I said to myself, 'If you can steal this much money all the time, why not just spend it on clothes and stuff rather than waste it on coke?'

"So that's what I did. I got into materialism, which is a habit just like drugs. All I wanted to do was buy more stuff. I stole another $300 from my mother the next day, but that's when she found out. We had a big fight over it. From then on I had to get my money somewhere else.

"Joe was in jail at the time. I was faithful to him, but I started going out with anybody who had money, which meant mostly drug dealers. I'd be going out with four or five guys at a time. I think I went out with every big-time dealer on the whole south side of town. I was four-teen years old and wearing a thousand dollars' worth of gold and riding around in limousines. I didn't really have any *relations* with them. I just used them until I got what I wanted, then dumped them.

"I wasn't really using drugs then. A lot of weed—maybe ten times a day—and beer or peach schnapps, but that was all. Most of the dealers didn't use either. The ones that did never had any money, and I wasn't inter-ested in guys with no money.

"I had to move out from my mother's house. We were always fighting. I was always high and sleeping all day and coming in at four in the morning. I got a job as a live-in baby-sitter for this lady whose name was Rose. She had two kids and was leading a pretty good life. At least she had enough money for food and rent. Her ex-husband used to beat her a lot, even when she was pregnant. Rose shot him a couple of years before I moved in. I don't know what ended up happening to him.

"Rose's kids always had on $50 suits and went to school very clean, hair combed and everything, and had three dollars in their pockets for milk and lunch. She took real good care of them.

"But the husband and wife living upstairs were dealing crack, and pretty soon Rose was doing it, too. And since she was using, she had to deal to get money. She got my friend Madeline to try it, and then *she* was hooked, too.

"I was trying to get Madeline to stop. She was completely different when she used. She didn't care about me or what I did or said. I didn't like her that way, but she was still my friend. Once she stopped for a couple of weeks, but then I caught her heating up a stem and getting ready to smoke. I said, 'Maddy, if you smoke that, I'm going out the door and I'll never talk to you again.' We'd been best friends for nine years. She said she didn't care and put it in her mouth. I got up and left. But I looked back and saw her take it from her mouth without smoking. I went back in. We had a big argument. But we were friends again.

"But another day, about two weeks later, the guy upstairs gave her a big rock of crack. For free, right? Of course it was too much of a temptation. I caught her smoking it. She'd just taken some into her mouth but wouldn't let the smoke out. I kept saying, 'You're smoking again, aren't you!' and she'd shake her head. I said, 'Open your mouth,' but she wouldn't do it until after a long time and there was no more smoke.

"Meanwhile, Rose was always trying to push it on me. I kept saying no, no, because I *knew* it was the next step for me. I'd done everything else.

"On July 15, two weeks after I turned sixteen, this guy I was going out with got shot and died. I couldn't believe it. I didn't know what to feel. I was smoking weed and pacing around Rose's living room, all torn up inside but not crying. Rose went out and bought me four 64-ounce bottles of beer. I drank them all in about four hours. Normally just a couple of cans of beer would get me drunk and put me to sleep. Now I was walking around, drunk but not sleepy. I kept saying, 'Why is this beer not doing anything to me? I don't like feeling like this.'

"Rose kept pushing the stem at me. I kept saying no, but after a while I just took it. Rose stuck the stem in my mouth, and I inhaled some. A few minutes later, I did some more, and then some more. Still I wasn't crying. I stayed awake all night. It wasn't until the next afternoon that I cried. I went to the place where he was shot. His blood was still on the ground. It was only then that I felt something and cried.

"That's when my life fell apart. I'd do anything for

crack. I *knew* it was bad and I was *real* ashamed of it. For a while my friends would tell me I had to stop, but I'd just hide somewhere and smoke it. They'd stop being my friends, and it wouldn't bother me at all. As long as I had that stem cooking in my hand, there was no problem with anything. Nothing mattered. Nothing. I knew it was bad and dirty and disgusting, but it just didn't matter. I'd smoke it and then sit there all scared and paranoid, and the next day I'd be completely depressed. I never went out looking for it though, or obsessing about it. But if somebody offered it to me, I just couldn't say no.

"Meanwhile, Rose was going straight downhill. I couldn't get her up in the morning. She was missing work and then got fired. Her beautiful kids were going to school in dirty clothes. They never took a bath. She was spending less than $20 a month on food. Just rice and canned beans and chicken. All her money went for crack. She was dealing, but she smoked too much of it and never had enough money for more.

"I think a woman on crack is the worst thing in the world. For men it's bad, but for a woman, it's the dirtiest, disgustingest thing in the world. A woman will sell herself. She'll do anything. She'll get as slutty as you can get. She'll be the dirtiest bitch in the world and not care. As far as I can see, crack is strictly a man's drug.

"I won't say I hate Rose, but if I saw her choking on a piece of meat, I wouldn't hit her on the back to save her. She doesn't matter to me any more. The thing that finally did it was when she went around telling everybody, including my mother, I was a slut because I was on crack. And it was her that made me start! When I found out she was telling everybody, I started beating on her. I really went nuts. I was trying to kill her with my bare hands. I would have, except some people dragged me off her.

"I was fighting all the time. Not just during the time I was on crack but also before. Three times was in the street. But I never fought when I was high. If I was on weed, I was too slow. If I was on coke, I just wouldn't care enough to fight about anything. I never lost a fight, and I didn't want to break my record, so I never fought when I was high.

"I got arrested four times, all while I was sixteen and seventeen years old. It was always for assault or disturbing the peace or failure to appear in court. Jail's about the worst place in the world. What some of the women in there do to each other is unbelievably bad. And I was sixteen years old. It was good I knew how to fight, that's all I can say. The longest I was in for was four months. I just learned to get used to it and to keep quiet and wait to get out.

"Madeline was getting worse and worse, too. Finally, one day I saw her die. She turned completely white and fell down dead. She stopped breathing, her heart stopped beating, and she went into convulsions. But after three minutes some ambulance guys managed to bring her back. That was enough for me. Right there, seeing my best friend fall down dead, I knew I wasn't going to touch crack again. Just like that, I stopped. I was seventeen at the time.

"Then Rose's house got raided. Madeline was living there and of course dealing. The people upstairs got sentenced to I don't know how many years. Madeline got offered a twenty-five-year sentence but was released on a promise to appear, which, of course, she didn't. She's out on the street now. I don't think she's using, but she's still out there acting crazy.

"Now I'm an in-patient in this program that's supposed to help young people get off drugs and finish school. I've stopped. No more crack. Never. Never, ever, ever. No way. Never. Now I live with my uncle and aunt. They're crackheads, but I watch them smoke, and I have no urge at all. I look at them and know how messed up it is.

"And no coke. I don't do coke except a couple of times I did just a *little* bit, enough that would fit on your fingernail, because I drank too much and didn't want to pass out. So no coke, except maybe. I don't *want* to use it, but I won't promise.

"And I don't drink hardly at all. Instead of every day, just one beer on a weekend every couple of weeks.

"And not much weed. Not like I used to, constantly, every day. That doesn't get you high. It just gets you stupid. Now I smoke a little, and it gets me high. My little cousins—they're eleven and twelve years old—like me when I'm high because I'm more fun. I offer them weed, but they won't take it. They're like just plain normal kids. While I was doing coke at their age, they're still playing with dolls. So I like to get high and play games with them and get into Loony Toons on TV and eat something and then just fall asleep.

"So basically, I'm trying to stay off drugs, but it's hard. My boyfriend and I are looking for an apartment because I know my uncle and aunt are going to get raided any day now. I'm going back to school at night to get my GED. I just have to keep hoping that things will stay normal, and who knows, maybe they will."

Questions about Cocaine and Crack

What happens when you use coke?

During initial use, cocaine produces feelings of exhilaration, energy, and alertness. With continued use, these pleasant feelings become short lived and less intense. With sustained use, the user may feel depressed, irritable, sleepy—yet unable to sleep. A typical response, then, is to increase the dosage or frequency of use. The high may be reached again, but with less intensity and more depression afterwards—"crashes." Eventually, prolonged use can lead to such serious mental problems as cocaine psychosis. Symptoms include paranoia, seeing, hearing, and feeling things, and apparent mental illness.

How is crack different from cocaine?

Crack is specially packaged cocaine. It comes in the form of small "rocks" of creamy color that are like pieces of rock salt. The term "crack" refers to the crackling sound it makes when it is smoked. It differs from cocaine powder in three ways:

> 1. It is smoked rather than sniffed. Smoking leads to a high in less than ten seconds, rather than one to two minutes. The high lasts less than fifteen minutes.

2. Because it is smoked, its effect is much more powerful than powder. The drug goes directly from the lungs to the brain.

3. It *seems* less expensive because it is sold in small quantities at a low price. However, since you use it more, it is actually more expensive in the long-run.

Why is crack so dangerous?

Crack quickly produces a high concentration of cocaine in the brain and bloodstream. Addiction tends to be quick, and medical problems can be serious.

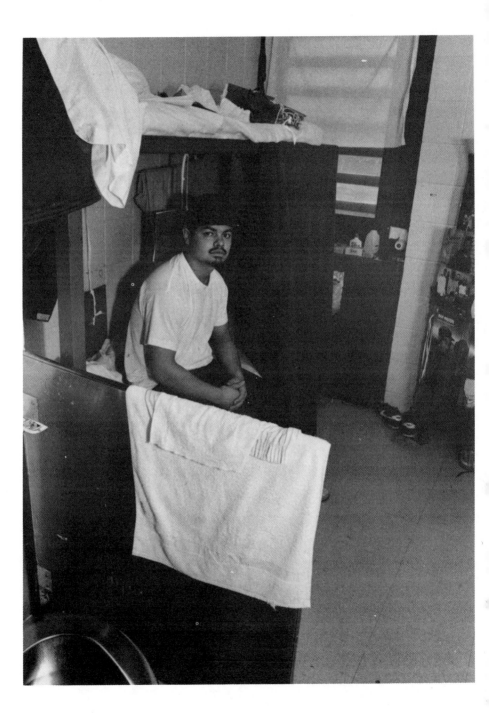

3

Roberto

Roberto, seventeen, used to live in a mixed-race neigh-
borhood in southern California. Now he lives in a
mixed-race youth correction facility. His father is Viet-
namese, his mother Phillipino. Roberto likes to dress in
stylish clothes that his peers will respect. In school, he
prefers English class and gym. His tastes in music lean
toward rap and jazz. His piercing black eyes look as
though they're always thinking about something. His
teachers usually believed him when he had some reason
for not going to class. He'd say he had to go to the of-
fice or bathroom or something but would go straight
outside to his van to take care of a certain business.

"I worked in a kennel until I got bit by a dog. My father felt sorry for me and said I could help him buy fruit
for his stand. But that meant getting up at four in the

morning, which just wasn't worth it. I mean I just couldn't do it.

"But I needed money. Without it, you're nothing. My mother used to give me a little, for a movie or something, but it wasn't enough to do anything special. I could take my girlfriend to a movie about every other week, but then one time this other guy took her shopping. He was a dealer, so he had bucks for all kinds of stuff. After that, she didn't want to know me.

"So it was like real obvious I had to start dealing if I was going to be anybody. I started looking out for a dealer, and pretty soon he was sending me and another kid into Los Angeles to get dope—heroin. All we had to do was hand over a certain envelope that had tape all around it, then bring home the envelope they gave us. I was very trustworthy, which of course I had to be or they'd kill me.

"That's how I learned the business. It paid enough for me to buy this old van. Me and another kid used to deal right out the window. I already knew a lot of customers, and they'd come to me because they knew I wouldn't rip them off.

"So I thought I was real cool. Very in control. I figured, okay, heroin's real bad. But coke's nothing. I can handle coke. Hell, I had the money, and there was this beautiful girl I knew who was really into it. So I sniffed with her. It was no big deal. No problem at all. It was great. I knew I could stop, so I figured I didn't have to.

"Trouble is, coke's *too* good. You can always use a little more. There's always a girl wanting to sniff with you. So I started dealing coke and dope both, and sometimes weed, too. They used to call my van The Supermarket. We put wood planks on the side that faced the street, to stop bullets, and had a hole in the floor for getting rid of stuff if we had to. We always parked over a sewer.

"I had this one girlfriend who was really my girlfriend. I could trust her. She stopped using when she was about fourteen. She smoked weed, that was all, so when I was with her, that's all I used. She wanted me to stop with coke, but I kept saying, 'Naw, I don't really use.'

"Then somebody told my father I was dealing. I came home about five in the morning. He was already up to go to work. He slammed me against the wall and said, 'You been selling drugs, boy?' He was spitting in my face when he said it. It smelled like toothpaste.

"I said, 'No way.'

"He said, 'How about if we go look in your van?'

"I didn't know what to say to that. I was just looking at him and thinking about killing him, which of course I would never do. He threw me in my room, shut the door, and called the police. They came and took the van and found everything in it, which, by luck, wasn't much. I went to court, but because I was only sixteen, they let me go to a special program instead of jail.

"The program was stupid. You have these group meetings and talk about how you don't use anymore. Everybody just lied. The ones who lied the best got out first. We had to do daily urine samples, too, which was easy. There was a clean kid who used to sell balloons with his urine in it. You go in the bathroom at the program and squirt a little clean urine into the jar and you come up clean.

"Trouble was, I was still using coke but didn't have money for it. I was afraid to deal because I was on probation. So I was a lookout for a while, and then a runner. But all my money went into coke. My girlfriend wouldn't even say 'hi' to me on the street. I always felt guilty when I saw her, and I always swore I'd stop. And maybe I would . . . for about three days—just enough to prove to myself that I could.

"A kid I knew who was just out of jail told me to go to a Narcotics Anonymous meeting. I told him I didn't have a problem. He told me if that's what I thought, I better go. I went, and it was just like in that other program. Everybody lying about how they almost use but then don't. I lied and told them I was ninety-eight days clean, and they all clapped their hands like idiots. I never went back.

"One day there was this kid who had a Mac 10 he bought cheap because it'd killed somebody. He said he'd trade it to me for my bullet-proof vest. I thought, hey, a gun's a gun. It was worth a lot more than the vest. We traded. Then I sold it to another guy for $500. And I *didn't* go right out and blow it on coke. I bought a Tech 9 and an Army issue .45 automatic from this girl whose boyfriend got shot and was in the hospital. She practically gave them to me. I was proud of myself for investing in something besides coke. I thought, 'See? You ain't hooked.' I sold the Tech and borrowed this old Caddy that nobody wanted. Then me and another kid took off for Los Angeles to see what we could find.

"First thing we did was score some coke and head back home. We were going to get rich. We had it all planned out. We were going to sell and buy more, sell and buy more, and not use any of it. We swore it. Then we took the next exit and did up a couple of lines right there on the ramp.

"And whadya' know but a State Highway Patrol cop shows up, and then about ten more. It was like they were waiting for us. There were cops all over the place and us lying on the ground. They found the gun, the coke, some weed, and of course the car, which it turned out was stolen before we borrowed it, which they didn't believe. And I was still technically on probation. They locked us both up and called our parents. The other kid's father came and made some kind of a deal. Mine said I could stay and learn a lesson. They did a urine test and found coke and marijuana in it, which was *barely* true. They said I could plead guilty to possession and grand theft and get two years or go hire a lawyer. I just said, 'Okay,' and here I am until I'm nineteen. They've got the same group meetings here as they do on the outside, and everybody tells the same lies. I tell them too. I can't wait to get out."

Questions about Cocaine

Can cocaine kill you?

Cocaine can lead to death in several ways. By forcing the heart to work harder and raising blood pressure, it can cause a heart attack. By overstimulating the body and brain, it can lead to extreme changes of body temperature. Extremely high fever or hyperthermia can kill the body. By affecting the electrical activity of the brain, it can lead to deadly seizures.

Activities associated with cocaine use also kill many users. Unsterilized needles can infect users with hepatitis B, blood poisoning, and AIDS. The psychological depression caused by cocaine use often leads to suicide. The illegal sources of cocaine and amounts of money involved often put users into violent situations.

Is it safe to snort cocaine?

Certainly not. Researchers have found that 80 percent of cocaine users seeking help were "only" snorting it. Virtually all of them were experiencing deteriorating health, including seizures, severe insomnia, visual difficulties, nausea and vomiting, severe headaches, and sexual problems, in addition to financial and social problems.

4

Robin

Robin comes from a town of blue-collar industrial work-
ers and white-collar commuters. For a good time, she
likes to go to a heavy metal concert. When she's home
alone and has nothing to do, she might listen to tapes
and write poetry. A bit on the short side, with big
brown eyes and lots of brown hair, she could be the hu-
man incarnation of Bambi. If you sat down for lunch in
the diner where she used to work as a waitress, you'd
probably leave her a nice tip. You'd never imagine her as
the type who could get so mad at the world that she'd
yank her hair out and scream about suicide.

"My drug of choice was marijuana. I first smoked it
at a friend's house. I'd been wanting to try it, mostly just
because I knew it was wrong. It was our freshman year in
high school. Some other kids gave us the joint. Until

years later, we didn't know it had coke in it, too. We smoked on her back porch. Everything was so mellow and slow. I loved the experience. I fell in love with the drug.

"I knew drugs were dangerous, but I wasn't going to get hooked. I knew about addiction, how addicts ended up shooting drugs in alleys, dropping out of society, and finally dying. As long as I was only smoking once a month, I wasn't an addict. I did it because it made me feel good and also because my parents tried to keep such a tight rein on me. I was in the sixth grade when I got drunk with a friend. We drank shots of everything that was in her parents' liquor cabinet. In junior high school I used to sneak out at midnight and go drinking until four in the morning with my older brother and sister and their friends.

"But pot was the best. It made me feel so good. When I smoked pot, I was a different person, and since I was a different person, I didn't have to be with myself. I really got to smoking a lot. From once a month it went to once a week, and then to once a day, and then all day long.

"I smoked before I got on the school bus, then hanging around the front of the school before it opened. Then between classes. School was the easiest place to get dope, get high, and be high. I never bought from a pusher or anything. Some kid would always have some. It was, 'You get me high today, I'll get you high tomorrow.'

We'd go out in the woods behind the school, in the dug-out at the baseball field, behind the maintenance shed. If a teacher caught us, he'd just make us go back inside. When we went into class late and all red-eyed, they never said a thing. When my grades dropped from high honors in grammar school to straight F's in high school, nobody but my parents seemed to notice.

"When I was fourteen, I was raped at a party where everybody was smoking and drinking. I knew the kid who did it, but that didn't make it any nicer. To help me get over the trauma, my parents put me in psycho-therapy for the next three years. Once the doctor asked me if I used drugs. I told him I didn't except for maybe a little pot now and then. And that was the end of the dis-cussion. It never came up again even though he knew I was violent and depressed and flunking at school.

"One day, my mother found a condom in my purse. She held it out in front of me and said What's this for.

" I said, 'What the hell do you think it's for?' I got real mad at her for going through my purse. We had a fight so bad I pushed her up against the wall. I found out she'd been searching my room and going through my di-ary. I'm still mad about that, but I can see how she had to do it for my own good.

"Pot wasn't making me mellow anymore. I got to hating everybody, and I was violent all the time. For no reason at all I'd all of a sudden throw a violent tantrum, punching holes in the wall, scratching myself, pulling my hair out, screaming that I was going to kill myself.

"My boyfriend was kind of psychotic, too. Neither one of us could get along in social situations, so we hung out together. I'd smoke at his house. I didn't know it at the time, but every joint he gave me had coke in it. I even smoked with his mother. I thought that was just as cool as you could get. But she was bad. I remember her yelling at her nephew, who was about four. At the time I thought the kid was a pain in the butt, but I remember him crying and coughing and his aunt smoking a joint and yelling at him to shut up. Now I feel real sorry for the poor kid.

"One day I smoked a lot of hash and a lot of grass and was about as high as I'd ever been. This was late in my sophomore year. I called my boyfriend and was telling him how high I was. I didn't know my mother was recording the whole thing on the answering machine. She came downstairs and said, 'Are you high?' Of course I couldn't deny it. But I was mad enough to kill her for taping my conversation. We had a fist fight. I punched her again and again. Even though she was deathly afraid of my violent tendencies, she finally got me calmed down. She took my pulse, and because she knew CPR, she decided my pulse was weak. So she took me to the hospital. They told her to take me home and let me sleep it off.

"That was the first time I knew my parents knew I

was on drugs, and all of a sudden I felt awful about it. I swore to myself I'd never, ever get high again. The next day I was totally depressed. I was crying, scratching myself from sheer hatred, thinking about suicide, writing poems, listening to heavy metal, all nervous and restless and just not knowing what to do. By afternoon I called my boyfriend and told him I needed to get high and I was coming right over.

"My mother tried to stop me from going out. We had a big fist fight. Then my father came home. He was real calm, like nothing had happened. He said he'd give me a ride to my boyfriend's because I shouldn't be walking alone when I got mad like that. So we got in the car. Then all of a sudden my mother got into the car, too. I immediately knew something was going on. I got real panicky. I yelled, 'Where are you taking me?'

"My mother said, 'County Hospital.'

"I knew what that meant. They had a psychiatric ward. That's where they took kids who really freaked out. A friend of mine was locked in there for seventeen days once for setting her father's car on fire. She said she saw people try to drown themselves in the toilet and burn themselves with cigarettes. They forced tranquilizers on you so you couldn't think.

"So I flipped out. No way was I going to County. I was pounding on both of my parents and screaming, 'I'm going to *kill* you! I'm going to *kill* you!' Then I said I was going to kill myself. I tried to strangle my mother with the seat belt. My father kept pushing me away until we were parked in front of the main door. Then he opened the back seat door.

"I refused to get out. A nurse tried to sweet-talk me, but there was no way I was going to get out. They called some big paramedics. They said I could come along peacefully or they could drag me out. Which did I want? I said I'd get out if they promised me that I could go back home that same day. They went and got a doctor, and he made the promise.

"So I went in. They did all kinds of tests on me. Urine. Blood. Everything. I acted real calm and rational. I kept telling the doctors and nurses that my parents were the crazy ones for thinking I was some kind of addict because I smoked pot. But one of the tests showed cocaine in my system. That's how I found out the pot I'd been smoking was laced. It shows how much you can trust your friends.

"They let me go home. First thing I did was break the answering machine tape in half. I was real mad about my mother doing that. My mother started having a nervous breakdown. She was rolling on the floor, rocking her head back and forth, saying, 'No, no, no' I looked down at her and said, 'You bitch, you deserve this.'

"But I wanted her to stop. Finally, I started apologizing and saying I'd never use drugs again. My father gave me a big hug. He was crying. He said it was the first time he'd cried since he was sixteen, when his father died. That's when I understood what I'd been putting them through. I knew it couldn't go on like this. Now I knew what the problem was, and I swore I'd never get high again.

"But I did. The next day. And then I knew I had to stop. But I got high again anyway.

"Finally, somebody I knew invited me to a Narcotics Anonymous meeting, and I agreed to go. It was weird when we got there. The meeting was down in the basement of a church. The lights were out, and candles were lit on a circle of tables. I thought, 'Oh great, a cult.' Most of the people in there were grubby-looking guys with beer bellies and tattoos, but there were a couple of women and a couple of people who looked like they wore ties to work. We were at the door and I was telling my friend, 'No way, no way am I going in there and tell a bunch of heroin addicts I'm a pot smoker.' But one of the addicts put his arms out and waved me in.

"I spent the whole time telling people I wasn't really an addict, I just smoked pot. But they didn't laugh. They told me they knew how I felt. They knew how hard it was to stop an addiction. They went around the table, each one talking about his or her problem. They'd start off saying, 'Hi, I'm Bob, or whatever, and I'm an addict,' and everybody would say, 'Hi, Bob.' Then I said the same thing, and they all said, 'Hi, Robin,' and for some reason, for some weird reason, even though it was just ritual, it felt good to hear it.

"They all told the same story: how they lacked any self-esteem, hated themselves, how they were so self-centered when they were on drugs. I couldn't believe there were people who felt just like I did. And at the coffee break, they put their arms around me and told me I could stop and that everything was going to be okay. After a couple of meetings, I admitted that I was an addict. That wasn't the end of it, but it was the first big step away from it.

"That was in May of my sophomore year. I went to meetings every week. I didn't drink or smoke anything after that except once in August. I've been clean since then. But that doesn't mean I haven't wanted to. I've wanted to smoke or drink almost constantly. I'm still afraid I'll start again. But I still go to meetings two or three times a week, even if I have to find a meeting in another town. If I went a week without a meeting, I'd be back on dope. I'm still an addict. It's funny, but I feel like if I ever use a drug again, I'll be letting down everybody who goes to those meetings. And, just about everybody does start using again. They use and get clean, use and get clean, over and over. We keep trying to help them, but it takes a long time.

"I have a sponsor who I can call any time of day or night if I think I'm going to lose it. She's been clean for over a year. When I catch myself rationalizing my way back to smoking, I call her. Sometimes I'll be thinking, 'Hey, I'm too young to stop partying,' or 'I wonder what it's like to take acid.' I call her if I'm dreaming about using. Once I dreamt I was Alice in Wonderland looking up at a giant mushroom. On top was that caterpillar smoking a hookah. Then I fell down a hole and couldn't get out. My parents were looking down the hole trying to reach me, but they couldn't. It's times like that when I need to talk to somebody.

"I'm a totally different person now. I don't get violent with my parents. I don't hate everybody. I don't hate myself. The biggest thing is that suddenly I know I have to be accountable for my actions. I have to be responsible. Where I used to be saying, 'I've got to get high now, while I'm young,' now I say, 'I've got to get my work done now, while I can.' My grades are back up to normal. I can go to a party and say no to a drink.

"We have meetings at school that are a little like the NA meetings. Kids who use drugs can get out of class to come talk about it. Some come just to skip class. Some of them come because they know they've got a problem. I'm always there to tell them what happened to me. I talk to the incoming freshman class, too. I figure some of them listen and learn, and some of them do like I did. They hear it and think, 'That'll never happen to me.' Then they go out and get high."

Questions about Marijuana

Why does marijuana make
a smoker feel high?

Marijuana contains a chemical called tetrahydrocannabinol, or THC, that prevents the brain from functioning normally. Its capacity to retain memory is greatly reduced. So is its ability to reason. Attention span, like memory, is short. It also loses part of its control over the body's coordination.

Can you overdose on marijuana?

Difficulty with tasks plus a short attention span and poor coordination is a formula for disaster. Though nobody ever smoked a deadly overdose of marijuana, uncountable thousands of users have ended up in the emergency room or dead after suffering an accident caused by their brain's limitations under the influence of marijuana.

Is marijuana addictive?

The body itself may not become physically addicted to marijuana, but the emotions and other mental functions can come to depend on it. This is known as psychological addiction. People who smoke a lot of marijuana need to smoke just to feel normal. Smoking is the only way they can stop feeling tired, sluggish, and depressed. As with other drugs, increased use leads to increased need and emotional instability. Heavy users can become moody and even violent in their frustration to perform normally. They might also become paranoid from fear of getting caught and from seeing others criticize their mental inadequacy.

Does marijuana have any harmful effects on the body?

Marijuana smoke harms the body as well as the brain. The body absorbs THC into its fatty tissues. The THC from a single joint may remain in the body for a week or more, slowly seeping into the bloodstream. If a smoker takes in THC several times a week, the chemical may remain in the body for a month, gradually attacking the body while the brain thinks everything is fine. Also, marijuana contains more carcinogens than cigarettes. One joint can do more damage to the lungs than a pack and a half of cigarettes. Long-term use has been associated with changes in the brain and blood cells.

5

Lauren

Lauren is a bit taller, a bit heavier, and a bit more intelligent than average. She kept herself busy in high school founding Young Republicans and, ironically, Students Against Drugs, volunteering at a hospital, serving as class treasurer, and participating in Sea Explorers. She has a big, wide-open baby face with small, quick, dark eyes. Something about her looks innocent and vulnerable, despite all she's been through. When she sits at a table and talks, her hands keep moving, though her wrists are always in contact with the table as if afraid to lose touch with it.

"The story of my addiction isn't much different from that of friends I had who were using. Addicts follow similar patterns. I am the only one of my old group who is in recovery. There is nothing special about my childhood or life that makes me different from anyone else. What separates me from most people is the disease of addiction.

"A large portion of my early memories are focused around drugs. Almost all of the adults I was in contact with—parents, friends' parents, neighbors—were involved in drugs. My fascination with drugs began early. I was obsessed with how it would feel to be high, how much it would change reality.

"My dreams about drinking became a reality when I was seven years old. I swiped beers out of people's refrigerators, one at a time, from anybody's house, as long as I could get away with it. I tried to get adults to let me drink from their beer cans. It was exciting, and it made me feel more mature.

"I was ten, in the fifth grade, the first time I smoked pot. I liked pot a lot better than drinking because it was easier. I loved it. I had a friend, Ginny, who started smoking around the same time. We got it from her older sisters. They liked to get us high on pot and alcohol.

"At about the same time, I was admitted into the Academically Talented program at school. I thought it was cool. I could be brilliant at school, then go home and escape from reality. I thought, 'Pot and alcohol, that's all I need. I don't want to get into anything else.'

"This was also about the time I started losing my interest in school. I blamed my behavior on my being so intelligent. I figured I could get away with anything.

When I entered junior high, they put me in the honors group. It was the first time I was with other smart kids. Instead of trying to keep up, I gave up. I started smoking pot in school as much as possible. I kept a bottle of Jack Daniels™ in my locker. My teachers used to ask me why I had to go to my locker so much.

"About this time I started getting obsessed with cocaine and thinking about what the high would be like. At the end of seventh grade, I tried it for the first time. My life changed completely with that first line.

"The thing that got me through middle school was the fact that there were drugs everywhere. I smoked in the bathroom during class and lunch and on the bus after school. I got to know everybody who used during the day, including a couple of guys, Charlie and Tony, who were sixteen and fourteen. Tony was dealing, so he always had enough coke for all of us. I was smoking at least two joints daily to ease the coke crash. About three to five times a week, we'd get buzzed on drinking. I had my second blackout on my fourteenth birthday. I didn't actually lose consciousness or anything, I just couldn't remember anything I had done over a certain time. From what other kids told me, I was just very volatile and acted like an obnoxious jerk.

"Near the end of seventh grade, Ginny got some acid. Being the type who has to go to extremes with everything, I couldn't take just one hit. I took three. It was a terrible trip. I was banging on some metal garbage cans with a hammer when a black and white cat came running over to me. I got scared and flipped out. I smashed it on the head and then beat it to death. Later I felt totally guilty and wanted to kill myself, too.

"I was abusive to people, physically and verbally. It was nothing for me to just walk up to somebody I didn't know or didn't like and punch them in the face. I told my teachers off whenever I could. Once I actually hit a teacher outside of school. I was at the height of a cocaine high when I did it. He hit me back, and I can't blame him. There was this kid who'd been in my class since fourth grade. I popped him in the face every chance I got. In the school library, I hit a girl in the face so hard I broke her nose. The blood spots are still in the carpet. Her parents called me and said they were going to sue, but I said if they did, I'd kill them. That was the last I heard of it.

"Once when I was smoking pot in the bathroom, my English teacher came in to get me. She was too stupid to notice. I said to another teacher, 'That stupid bitch didn't even realize I was smoking a joint in there,' and he said to me, 'I think you have a serious problem with drugs and alcohol.' I just laughed and said I was too young. But by the end of that year, I would just break out a mirror and do lines at my desk in the classroom.

"The end of eighth grade was one of the worst times of my life. I didn't just snort cocaine. I also snorted crack and took speed orally. I was suicidal; there was no question about it. I thought about it and talked about it a lot. My first attempt at suicide was that April. I was at a friend's house. They had a garage, which my house didn't. I saw it as an opportunity. I closed all the doors and started the car. I sat in the front seat, happy because I was going to die. My friend's brother found me, though, and all I ended up with was a bad headache.

"That night I went on a cocaine binge. The next day I was so strung out I couldn't go to a state industrial arts conference where I'd entered a Computer Aided Design project. I was in the nurse's office when my adviser showed up and handed me the first place trophy.

"I went on to win the regionals, too. The school won a bunch of computer equipment that I was supposed to use to enter the national competition. It was like I had immunity from everything. If I won the nationals, the school would get $20,000 worth of computer equipment.

"I started taking more and more speed to give myself energy to work on the nationals project. I was taking gobs of diet pills another kid stole from his mother. Before gym I'd line up crystal meth on a mirror for my friends, and we'd all snort it for extra energy. I decided to try LSD again. Just like last time, my friends tried to get me mad so I'd do something crazy. They succeeded. I had a fight with Ginny so bad I pinned her to the floor and had a kitchen knife at her throat. I would have killed her,

I really would have if her boyfriend hadn't dragged me off.

"The night the winners were announced, I had to wait three hours before they got to announcing my event. I came in fourth place out of fifteen contestants. I thought I should be happy with that, but I wasn't. Since everyone at home had told me I'd win, I really thought that I would. After we left, I was trying to keep myself from being disappointed, but my mother was pissed that everyone had psyched me up for success and I had lost. I started crying and told her I didn't need to hear that. I was disappointed enough at that point. I couldn't help but feel like I hadn't worked hard enough at the drafting, but I still felt honored to have made it to the national level.

"After eighth grade my parents sent me to a private girls' school. I was psyched. I was going to change my life, develop a new reputation, really get my act together. But it wasn't long before I found the girls who were doing drugs. They didn't know much about it, though, so once I sold them coke so cut with aspirin it hardly did anything. Then I sold some muscle relaxant to a girl who ended up having seizures and going to the hospital. That was the last time I sold drugs to anybody at that school.

"I was doing coke and pot and alcohol as much as ever, but no more speed, when I did three weird things. I joined the Explorer Scouts because of all the field trips. I organized Young Republicans for George Bush and campaigned for him door-to-door. And I founded Students Against Drugs.

"I managed to balance those activities with heavy-duty drug and alcohol use because I have two separate personalities: one that can act perfectly straight, one that wants to get trashed. I can talk to jocks, brains, and drug addicts equally easily.

"When Bush won the election, he invited me to attend the inaugural ball. It was the biggest thing that had ever happened in my life. I got a special gown and everything, and I went to Washington. My parents kept telling me up until I got on the plane that I didn't have to go if I didn't think I could handle it. It was all set, though. I had taken my midterms at school a week earlier because I would have missed them. The only thing I was nervous about was going away without drugs. I didn't take any drugs with me because I was afraid of getting searched on the plane. The night before the ball all I could think about was how bad I needed coke. I ended up flying home before the ball. My parents were in shock. They knew how much the ball meant to me. That's when they figured out I really had a problem. They took me to a mental health clinic, where they figured out I was depressed but didn't see any drug problem because I didn't tell them about how much I used.

"Fifty kids joined Students Against Drugs. I had them believing that I used to use but had kicked the habit. I gave speeches about my miraculous recovery. I was also yelling at Charlie, Ginny's boyfriend, to stop using, and I was trying to keep Ginny from going out with him because he was nineteen and she was only fifteen and would do anything he told her, such as using coke. So one night he came over to my house really, really drunk. I was relatively sober. I refused to share the Jack Daniels™ he had under his coat and told him he was disgusting and was ruining his life.

"That was the last time I saw him alive. A week later he booked into a motel room and free-based coke until he had a massive heart attack. When I heard, I knew immediately he'd done it on purpose—that it was suicide.

"That week I smoked crack for the first and only time. I called Tony—Charlie's brother—to get high after an Explorer Scout meeting. He took me to a crack house in Springfield. It was an incredible dump in the middle of a ghetto. Roaches were crawling all over the place. The smell was terrible. It reminded me of my childhood, when my parents used to free-base. One guy in there thought I was a narc and pointed a gun at me, but Tony cooled him down. The crack got me real high real fast, but after three or four minutes, it was gone. I thought, 'That's it?' I told the dealer I wanted more, but he said no, I had to pay from then on. I didn't have any money, so that was the end of it.

"I still didn't think I was an addict. I actually thought you couldn't get addicted to just line cocaine, and I told myself I could stop any time I wanted. It just happened I didn't want to.

"I shot up with a needle a few times with some older guys who lived together down the street. I used their needle, which they cleaned by running plain tap water over it. Of course, I wasn't thinking about AIDS at the time, but now I have to worry. They used heroin, too. I wanted them to give me some, but they wouldn't. For some reason giving heroin to a fifteen-year-old was bad while helping her shoot coke was okay.

"I had Charlie on my mind all the time, and that winter of my sophomore year, I did a lot of free-basing. Around Christmas time I decided I wanted to commit suicide, too. I was very methodical and scientific about it. I wrote a suicide note and sharpened my favorite knife. I laid out a few lines of coke on the kitchen table and fixed two pots of water: one cold, one hot. The cold was to numb my wrist. The hot was to keep the blood flowing faster.

"I snorted the lines, stuck my left arm into the cold water, and lit a cigarette. As soon as my arm was numb, I made a deep cut into my wrist. Then I sat on the kitchen floor with the phone, stuck my arm into the hot water, and called a friend. I tried to make like there was nothing wrong, but I told her I was thinking about committing suicide. She got all excited and made her father drive her through a snowstorm to my house. By then the bleeding had stopped. I wore long-sleeve shirts for a long time after that. My parents never knew.

"At the end of my junior year, I got thrown out of the girls' school for vandalism. Public school turned out to be a better place to get high and stay high. By this time I was really falling apart. I had to put Preparation H™ suppositories up my nose to stop the swelling the coke caused. I had nosebleeds all the time and a terrible headache from morning until night. Sometimes somebody could talk to me for twenty seconds before I noticed. My parents sent me to the doctor to see if I was having seizures. I had a CAT scan, an EEG, the works. But they never figured out what the problem was. It never occurred to me the problems were drug-related. When they asked if I used drugs, I said no, and that was the end of it. They put me on an antidepressant, which stopped the headaches.

"Meanwhile, I was leading what looked like a normal life. I had jobs in a restaurant and a gas station and painted houses. I was a volunteer in the cancer center at the hospital. I was elected treasurer of my class.

"It was only in my senior year that I finally began to accept that cocaine was causing all these problems. I still didn't think I was addicted. Even though I knew I should stop, I never did. A teacher at school told me to join a student discussion group that met to discuss their use of drugs. I was surprised to find out I used a lot more than any of them. I thought everybody else was like me.

"After that, I started using more coke than ever. I'd try to come as close to death as possible. I'd feel my heart freeze, just *stop*. I'd lose consciousness and cough up white foam. Even when I wasn't real high, I'd black out or get chest pains and cough up clots of blood. A rehab counselor visiting our group said, 'I've seen kids like you before and they usually end up dead.'

"In October of my senior year, I started going to Narcotics Anonymous, but it didn't do me much good. It was a struggle just to go a few days without coke. I'd be real proud of myself if all I did was drink whisky and smoke pot. By November I was using coke again, but I still went to meetings. I was kidding myself that I was quitting.

"From the discussion group at school, my counselor knew I was running out of time. He called my mother in and told her I needed in-patient rehabilitation therapy immediately. She agreed to send me to a rehab place out of state. I spent two weeks there. It was like a prison, with every move strictly regimented. We wore uniforms, did chores, smoked cigarettes only on breaks. You can't keep a journal or call home. My roommate was a girl who'd been on crack since she was eight years old.

"Every minute of every day was related to drug and alcohol abuse: movies, AA meetings, discussions. I had to fill out a Chemical History detailing every drug I'd ever taken, how often I took it, and how much I figured I took in my whole life. I went back to the fifth grade. It came out to about 51,000 ounces of alcohol, 4,000 joints, 1,000 grams of coke, 9 hits of LSD, 1,500 pills of speed, 4 hits of crack, 8 bottles of White Out, and 40 tablets of Vivarin and 8 tablets of No-Doze.

"After two weeks I wanted to leave. I had to sign a contract agreeing not to use, to attend AA or NA meetings, and go meet with a counselor every week. They tried to talk me out of going. They said I'd be dead in a month if I left. A shrink showed me an EKG that indicated I'd have a heart attack if I used coke again.

"I was out for a month and thinking about getting high *all* the time. I decided to go to another rehab program. I got into one closer to home. It wasn't so strict, but after two weeks, I left. For a long time I went to NA meetings every night. Now, I've been clean for a year, but I still go to NA meetings three or four times a week even if it means going to another city to find one. I leave for college in Colorado next week. I already have my first meeting scheduled there. I know I can't stop going to those meetings. If I went a week without them, I'd start again. I'm real worried about college. I know it's going to be a heavy party scene. Somebody's going to push a beer at me. And, if I take it, I'll start drinking again, and then I'd start doing coke again, and probably die."

Questions about Addiction

How do I know if I'm addicted to a drug?

There are many warning signs. Just one or two in a given individual is enough to indicate a serious problem or addiction. Here are some of the signs:

- You leave or skip school to look for drugs.

- You hide your drug use from friends.

- You use drugs to cope with a problem such as shyness, anxiety, insomnia, or depression.

- You think ahead to where you'll find more drugs or more money to buy drugs.

- You use before you get into a situation where you plan to use, like having a drink before you go to a party where you know there will be drinking.

If I am really addicted, is there any hope for me?

Yes, but there's no quick cure. You can stop using, but you'll probably always want to use again. Few addicts manage to stop the first time they try. Recognize that you will experience setbacks along the way, and find a drug counselor and program that will help you. *The first step is to ask for help.*

How can I help a friend who uses drugs too much and too often?

First, you have to tell your friend that you think he or she has a problem. Then encourage the user to ask for help. Don't make it easier for the user by lending money, caring for a child, cleaning up after him or her, or asking others to excuse your friend's behavior. Ask a drug counselor for advice on the best way to handle your friend's particular situation.

I have a parent who is an addict. Does that mean I am genetically destined to become an addict?

There is a possibility that you will have a genetically inherited tendency to use drugs and become addicted. Knowing this, you should realize that your use is a major risk. If you never use for the first time, however, you cannot become addicted.

6

Miles

Quick to let out a laugh, Miles always looks as though he's got a joke in the back of his mind. He likes school, especially math and history. Miles is African-American, and he likes rap music and Ray Charles. Though he's only fifteen years old, he knows the feeling of carrying a large caliber semiautomatic pistol and a few thousand dollars under his bulletproof vest. He also knows what it feels like to hear stray bullets whiz past his head, to have handcuffs around his wrists, and to realize there's something very wrong with his life.

"I started smoking weed when I was eleven. Before that, I thought weed and cigarettes were the same thing. Where I live, which is in the bad part of town, you can smoke weed on the street and no cop's going to give you problems unless you like rub it in his face.

"When I was younger, my father let me try smoking a cigarette. Of course I hated it, so I never wanted to smoke. But I was hanging around with older kids, and one day one of them said, 'Hey, let's smoke some weed,' so I did. I liked it, and pretty soon I was smoking more and more. I smoked all day, starting early in the morning. Pretty soon it was weed with embalming fluid and angel dust. It keeps you high for four or five hours. Everything seems to slow down so you can see it in detail. That's what happened with me, anyway. Some people just go crazy.

"I live in a real bad part of town. I seen a lot of bad things. When I was about seven, I come out of the movies with my mother, and there was a guy who got his leg shot off. He was crawling down the street without his leg. He got up to the corner and died next to a trash can. I seen a young girl die of AIDS because she was willing to sell her body to buy dope. I was waiting for a bus one day, and there was a fight down the street. Some kid beat up a man so the man took out a gun and shot at the kid, and then the kid pulled out a gun. Bullets were going *zoop, whee-oo,* past my head. I was just about to dive into a phone booth when a bullet hit the dial, and it flew into the air. If I'd been there one second sooner, the bullet would have hit me.

"I was twelve when I started dealing coke. I didn't actually sell the stuff, though. I had other kids do it so I wouldn't have to hold it. I'd just be there watching the street, smoking and making sure nobody tried to run off. I always had guns—.44's, pumps, Macs, and I always wore a vest. Vests don't always work though. They won't stop a .44.

"I used to hang out with my older brother. We had a reputation. Nobody would mess with us. One kid punched my brother, so he smoked him. We just rode off on our bikes and left him bleeding. They arrested my brother, put him in detention for a while, then let him go on house arrest. The kid who punched my brother lived, and later came back to apologize because he was scared.

"My brother and I were real close. I have three older sisters, too, but they're straight, and I didn't have much to do with them. My father ran off a long time ago. My mother's straight, too. She works at a college. She always says I'm going to turn out like my brother, which she means as not good. He and I'd always be out having a good time. We did anything we wanted.

"My brother was arrested for killing somebody when he was fourteen. A guy pulled a knife on him, so he had to kill him. He got nine years. When it happened, I went on a rampage. I was crazy mad. A kid slapped me in school the next day, and I hit him so hard I knocked him out. I got in a fight with a teacher.

"I was dealing a lot then and making crazy money. I'd have $4,000 or $5,000 on me at the end of the day. It wasn't all mine, of course. I had to pay a lot of people.

One of my girlfriends was always saying, 'You gotta cut that out,' but I just said, 'Naw, I ain't gonna get caught.'

"But they got me for possession. I was just running across a field to take some coke over to the projects. But a kid had stolen a car near there, and the police saw me running and thought I'd jumped out of it. So I'm running across the field thinking, 'Why they chasin' *me*? Why they chasin' *me*?' They found coke on me and $600.

"I was fourteen then. It was my first offense, so they let me go on probation. But I didn't think there was anything wrong with being on probation and smoking a little weed. Then, they arrested me again for possession. They asked me if I wanted to stand trial or plead guilty to a lesser charge. I knew they'd find me guilty if I went to trial, so I had to take the plea. Then they gave me the choice of jail or a rehab place. I knew from my brother that jail wasn't cool, so I took the rehab.

"It's not too bad here. I come every day after school. We have group sessions. They make you think. We talk about how to have control over your life and how to think about something before you do it and how to have the courage to say no to drugs. I don't smoke any more. Now I know how it keeps you from being smart. I always thought I was real smart when I was high, but I think a lot better when I'm not.

"I learned that you got to slow down or you get killed. There's been crazy killing going on. I know a *lot* of kids who got shot. Elvis. Davey. Somebody's dead body got dumped in the trash. So I'm just chilling now. I stay home all the time. No more trouble for me.

"I want to be a lawyer someday so I always will have a lot of money. I'm going to marry a smart girl and have smart kids. I'm going to tell them the truth. I'm going to tell them, 'Hey, there's drugs out there. You get high, you're fooling with your life.' But they'll do like I did when my mother told me things. They'll just do what they want. I just hope they figure out what they're messing with before it's too late."

Questions about Drugs
and Urban Life

Is drug abuse a good predictor of whether someone will engage in criminal activity?

While drug abuse is not an exclusive indicator of a "life of crime," many law enforcement officers, especially in major cities, consider a personal history of drug abuse to be an important predictor of serious criminal activity.

Do drug users turn to a life of crime to support their drug habits, or do drugs harden existing criminals?

Although the exact connection between drugs and crime is questionable, there seems to be evidence to support the claim that a connection does exist. So, in the end, discouraging drug abuse would appear to be a good preventative measure.

What role do gangs play in the drug problems in our cities today?

Young and increasingly violent drug gangs are waging brutal territorial battles to terrorize neighborhoods. The gangs often want to eliminate rivals, discourage informers, and do whatever it takes to keep the law-abiding citizens of the neighborhood from complaining about the drug trafficking.

7

Marcia

Marcia was born in Puerto Rico but came to Miami when she was thirteen. Fluent in English and Spanish, she was an excellent student, earning almost straight A's until she reached the tenth grade. She even attended university courses during the summer. In her spare time, she liked to read novels about people in love. As a member of various Hispanic clubs at school, she was busy and popular. She went to church and loved to go on retreats. A fan of the same pop music that everybody else listens to, she never missed a school dance. For her first fifteen years, she looked like the classic case of a working-class student bound for college and success.

"I was a good student and a very straight kid until I was fifteen. Then for some reason I thought it would be cool to drink. I guess I thought it made me special some-how, like it made me stand out from all the other kids. What's strange is that my father drank a lot until I was nine. He was responsible enough to bring home enough money for the family, but he was always out drinking. Sometimes he got kind of violent, too. It amazed me how he suddenly stopped and became a different person. What's weird is that I didn't see the same thing happening to me. Now I know that my family history was a big factor in all my problems.

"So anyway, I started hanging out with kids who thought about drinking all the time. We'd sneak out of school, and one of the older kids would get a bottle of rum and we'd all get drunk. Pretty soon I was smoking cigarettes and then marijuana just because everybody else was. It all came at once.

"My attitude toward school changed totally. It didn't matter to me anymore. I didn't care if I finished my work or even if I flunked.

"Around that time I fell in love with a boy who had dropped out of school and left home when he was four-teen. His father was an alcoholic, and his mother had fif-teen kids. He was real tough, a real survivor who knew how to live on the streets. He drank and used cocaine, but he was a caring person, and he cared about me. We really understood each other. I was totally in love. And pretty soon I was pregnant.

"In my culture, a girl is supposed to be a virgin until

she gets married. My parents were really mad at what happened. They made Tommy come in and explain how he was going to care for me and my baby. He just said he'd marry me, and that's what we did. I was pregnant at my high school graduation and was a mother before I was eighteen.

"Tommy was working nights as a machine tool operator in a factory. I never saw him. The job was killing him and our marriage and our family. But I did manage to get pregnant again, and we just didn't have enough money to support another kid. Tommy saw guys on the street making hundreds of dollars a day, so he decided that was the only way we'd ever have time to be together and feed two kids.

"It was weird having people come to the house all the time looking for coke. I couldn't handle it, so I started using, too. It was easy because we always had a lot of it. But coke makes you get real hyper, so we started using heroin to calm down. Using both is what everybody calls the 'Rich man's high.'

"We started dealing heroin to make more money, but it didn't work. We'd always buy a lot and figure we were going to double our money, but we ended up using it all ourselves. So we had to go out and steal. I'd take the two kids and go steal stuff from stores and also from my parents. Sometimes I'd leave the kids at home, a four-year-old baby-sitting a one-year-old, while I went out to find dope.

"Pretty soon I was smoking crack so I could really feel the high. I was totally addicted, totally dependent on the two drugs. Tommy was mad at *me* for using, but he was using, too. He thought *I* had the problem. When we needed money bad, I'd go out and stick somebody up, which he was afraid to do. That made me real proud, like I was independent or something.

"Meanwhile, we kept getting kicked out of apartments because we didn't have the rent. I kept thinking that if we moved to another place, we'd leave our trouble behind. The trouble was, I always took myself where I went, and I was the problem. But I didn't know that. I thought I was doing fine. I thought the world was mine and I could do whatever I wanted, and everybody else was just there to give me problems. I hated my parents because they said they wanted to help me but wouldn't give me any money. They kept trying to get us into programs. We started a few programs—methadone and such—but as soon as we finished, we'd start again and get even worse.

"When I look back on it, I see that we didn't have *knowledge* about our addiction. We didn't know it was normal for addicts to think they could stop any time and that they didn't really have a problem. I didn't know that a tendency to get addicted can be passed down from a parent to the kids.

"When I got pregnant for the third time, my baby was addicted even before he was born. When I needed drugs, he needed them, too. He'd kick around inside me until I got another fix. When I went to the hospital, I had to tell the doctors I was using. It was too late in the pregnancy to stop, so they gave me methadone.

"When Ricardo was born, his feet were deformed, and he went into withdrawal because he wasn't getting any more drugs through me. It took him two months to detox. He cried all the time for no reason except that his body wanted heroin. He shivered a lot, had constant diarrhea, and would throw up almost everything he ate. Tommy wasn't there because he was in jail for dealing.

"I felt so guilty I wanted to die, but I didn't have the courage to kill myself. A week after I got out of the hospital, I started drinking. That reactivated my disease and led me right back to the drugs. After that, I couldn't even take care of my own kids. When my oldest was ready for kindergarten, I was too sick every morning to get her off to school. More than anything, I wanted her to get a good education, so I just left her at my mother's house. I kept the other two with me, but I didn't take care of them at all.

"Finally, me and the kids got arrested together. Tommy was already in jail, so the cops took me and some dope I had and the kids all to my parents' house. Then they took me to jail. For the first time, my parents refused to help me. They left me there all night. It was like the whole world fell on top of me. I knew it was all over. I knew I wasn't a kid anymore and I had to stop.

When my father finally came to bail me out, I knew I wasn't going to use anymore.

"But it wasn't easy. I couldn't get into a program, so I had to detox at home. It was like hell for a whole week. It felt like death coming on. I had hot flashes and cold chills, and all my bones and muscles hurt real bad. I couldn't sleep even though I was so weak I could hardly get up. The anxiety was terrible. I thought I was going to die if I didn't get some drugs into me. If I'd had the strength, I might have gone to look for some.

"I found a program just for Latinos, but there was a three-week wait. They already started working on me, though, by having me come in all the time with urine samples and making me read stuff about addiction and write about my feelings. It kept me busy. More than anything in the world, I wanted to use again, and at the same time, more than anything in the world, I never wanted to live that kind of life again. It was a constant battle in my head, pulling me both ways at the same time.

"When I finally started the program, I was the only girl among seventeen guys. I was afraid, but they were really nice to me. They really understood what I was going through, and they really tried to help me. They helped me understand the first step I had to take, which was to realize that my life was out of control. That was totally true.

"I learned a lot of other things. I learned that I'm a

winner because I don't use. I learned that addicts have two personalities: one that wants to use and one that doesn't. I also learned that my father's been in recovery for sixteen years. I learned to deal with life as it is and not try to hide from it. Even when reality looks ugly, it's beautiful. I can see it for what it is and I can cope with it, and there's nothing more beautiful than that."

Questions about
Drugs and Pregnancy

Can a baby become addicted before it's born?

Yes. Since the mother and her fetus share the same blood, they share the same nutrients and the same drugs. Like all drug addicts, they suffer withdrawal symptoms once they are born and stop sharing the same bloodstream and drugs with their mother.

Does the use of marijuana during pregnancy have any harmful effects on the baby?

Studies have shown that babies born to mothers who smoked marijuana during their pregnancy tend to weigh about a half a pound less than normal. In some cases, babies suffer tremulousness, or low sensitivity to light, and abnormally high-pitched screaming—all similar symptoms of infant withdrawal from heavier drugs.

What is fetal alcohol syndrome?

Even moderate drinking during pregnancy is transferred to the baby through a shared bloodstream. Whatever you drink while pregnant, your baby drinks, too. This can lead to birth defects. Babies born to mothers who drink while pregnant tend to be shorter and lighter, with smaller heads, eyes, mouths, and jaws. Cleft palates (holes in the roof of the mouth) are relatively common.

Babies often suffer heart defects, including holes in internal heart walls. Alcohol shared between the mother and child's bloodstream may also cause mental retardation, sleep disturbance, and hyperactivity.

How does smoking cigarettes while pregnant affect the fetus?

Cigarette smokers inhale concentrated doses of carbon monoxide, the same poisonous gas found in car exhaust fumes. Carbon monoxide combines with red blood cells to make them less capable of carrying oxygen to the body and, in the case of a pregnant woman, the fetus. Consequences can include premature birth and lower birth weight.

Epilogue

Nobody really knows why people start using drugs. Nor does anyone know why some people stop while others go on into addiction. Theories abound, but none of them explains all patterns of drug use. Biologists have found evidence of genetic causes, but sociologists often point to social causes, and psychologists tend to lay much of the blame on what they term an "addictive personality."

It would be a dangerous oversimplification to link all drug use to a single cause. But a few general tendencies seem to indicate some of the causes of first use and eventual addiction.

Very often drug use is handed down from parent to child, almost like a tradition. In some cases, the tendency toward addiction may be a biologically inherited trait. In others, it may be learned behavior, with children naturally assuming that their parents lead a normal life.

The tendency to begin and continue using drugs may be founded in personality. Psychologists have detected a common trait among addicts: virtually all of them suffer from low self-esteem. For some reason, drug use seems to work as a mental crutch that helps them overcome feelings of inadequacy.

In a related explanation, some people use drugs to overcome such temporary mental states as stress, depression, boredom, fear of criticism, and feelings of guilt. The drug may give the user a sensation of power, exceptional ability, or confidence.

Most often, first use, if not actual addiction, is socially inspired. It's natural to do what their peers do and to be accepted by society. If the society around an individual encourages drug use, the individual is faced with the choice of being accepted or rejected by society. It's not easy to choose rejection.

The social aspect is especially powerful during adolescence. In this highly social stage of life, teens strive to fit in, to do what everybody else is doing, to be cool. As is natural for people their age, they tend to discredit warnings and disobey authority. Teens are in a hurry to grow up and start doing the things adults do. They're curious about new things and innocent about how serious some things can be.

The advice of parents, teachers, and other authority figures is to "Just say no," but a lot of other factors seem to say, "Go ahead, do it." Billboards put cigarettes—one of the most addictive drugs—in glamorous situations. Magazine advertisements associate alcohol—considered the most dangerous and widely abused drug—with success, happiness, status, and sex. Television commercials mix beer and friendship. Stores sell paraphernalia for using illegal drugs. Adults in movies, soap operas, and real life drink and smoke and even use the same illegal drugs they tell their children not to use. Meanwhile, none of these sources of information shows much, if anything, about the negative side of drug use.

A high school drug counselor at a high school in Connecticut says that much of America's drug abuse problem is supported by and perhaps even caused by the nature of our society. In the modern American economy, it's all too easy to believe that you can buy happiness, that satisfaction can come as quickly as fast food, that there's an instant cure for everything. When a kid first tries a drug, it all seems true. For $10 or $20, you can forget your sadness or poverty or messed-up relationship. To feel satisfied with yourself and your life, all you need to do is find some dope. And if you do get hooked, a quick rehab program will straighten you out.

But life isn't like that. Drug-induced euphoria often turns into dreadful depression. The feeling of satisfaction turns sour. Recovery takes a lifetime and is never really complete. Most users never stop using for long.

No one ever first takes a drug with the intention of becoming addicted. Everyone thinks, "It can't happen to me." The person experiences the pleasure that drugs offer at first. Naturally, having seen how easy it was, he or she uses it again. This is the early stage of addiction. It can really seem rather fun.

But it's also rather dangerous. With each use, the users build up a tolerance to the drug. They need more to experience the same feelings. Pretty soon they find themselves thinking about it as they look forward to the next chance to use. They are no longer using the drug for pleasure but only to keep themselves out of the depression or withdrawal that results when they don't have the drug.

Something about the mental process of addiction makes it impossible for the addict to admit he or she has a problem. In a state known as "denial," the addict not only refuses to recognize the problem but also consciously justifies use as voluntary and harmless.

The addict—and alcoholics are included in this group—eventually starts feeling guilty. Efforts to abstain repeatedly fail as the addict thinks up amazingly imaginative excuses for use and alibis for certain behavior he or she isn't proud of. As the drug becomes more important, the addict loses interest in work, friends, and any fun not involving drug use. A perceptible pattern begins in which the addict lands in unwanted and unforeseen situations—humiliating situations, accidents, arrests, violence, blackouts, loss of job, broken relationships.

In the final stages of addiction, the body, mind and emotions begin to break down. Increasingly unable to function in society, the addict "bottoms out." Sometimes the bottom is the realization that life is out of control and something needs to be done. Sometimes, however, the bottom is death.

When Someone Needs Help

At some point in your life, you will probably know someone who is getting too seriously involved in a drug. You may notice increasing use and obsession or merely a change in behavior. If you're a friend, you may notice the addict has found a new friend, the kind bought in a liquor store or on a street corner. But this is no time for you to abandon a friendship. It's time for you to offer help. Normally an addict will not recognize his or her problem. But the sincere advice of a friend may be enough of a hint. Don't expect to solve the problem yourself. Just get your friend to seek help.

You may suspect that you yourself have a problem. Because chronic drug use causes the mind to play psychological tricks, it's hard, or even impossible, to recognize your own addiction. You can see many symptoms in the teens profiled in this book. Addicts tend to gradually increase the amount they use. They think about and plan and look forward to using in the near future. They constantly deny, to themselves and others, that they have a problem. Their use leads to a pattern of landing in situations where they don't want to be.

If you have a friend who seems to need help, or if

95

you even *suspect* you yourself need help, you should get information so you can make intelligent decisions.

Look in your local telephone book for any of the following agencies or organizations. All you have to say is, "I'd like information about addiction to [the drug in question]." Or you can just say you need help.

In the white pages, look for Alcoholics Anonymous, Narcotics Anonymous, Cocaine Anonymous, Al-Anon, or Teen-Anon. If you have a family member or friend who needs help but refuses to seek help, contact the organization yourself and ask for advice.

In the blue pages (government listings), look for a department of health, mental health, or human services. If your phone book has no blue pages, look in the white pages under the names of your town and state.

In the yellow pages, look under "Social Services."

You can also call one of the following toll-free national hotlines:

> National Institute on Drug Abuse
> Information and Referral Line
> 1-800-662-HELP
> Monday—Friday, 8:30 A.M.—4:30 P.M.
> (Eastern Standard Time Zone)
>
> National Council on Alcoholism
> 1-800-622-2255
> 7 days a week, 24 hours a day

Cocaine Hotline
1-800-COCAINE
Monday—Friday, 9:00 A.M.—3:00 A.M.
(Eastern Standard Time Zone)
Saturday—Sunday, Noon—3:00 A.M.
(Eastern Standard Time Zone)

"Just Say No" Club Hotline
1-800-258-2766
Monday—Friday, 8:00 A.M.—5:00 P.M.
(Pacific Time Zone)

Bibliography

Dozens of books have been written on substance abuse, addiction, and recovery from addiction. A few titles are listed below. A librarian or bookstore salesperson can help you find other books, and a drug counselor can recommend others. In your library card catalog, look under "Drug Abuse."

Barrymore, Drew., *Little Girl Lost.* New York: Pocket Books, 1990.

Becker, Robert A., *Don't Talk, Don't Trust, Don't Feel.* Deerfield Beach, FL: Health Communications, 1991.

Black, Claudia., *It Will Never Happen to Me.* New York: Ballantine Books, 1991.

Gold, M.D., Mark., *The Facts About Drugs and Alcohol.* New York: Bantam, 1986.

Grinspoon, Lester and Bakalan, James., *Cocaine: A Drug and Its Social Evolution.* New York: Basic Books, 1985.

Haury, Don., *I'm Not at Fault.* Scottsdale, AZ: Safe Place Publishing, 1990.

Kellogg, Terry., *Broken Toys, Broken Dreams.* Little Elm, TX: Brat Publishing, 1990.

Monroe, Judy., *Stimulants, Hallucinogens.* New York: Macmillan, 1991.

Robinson, Byron., *Heal Your Self-Esteem: Recovery from Addictive Thinking.* Deerfield Beach, FL: Health Communications 1991.

Turck, Mary C., *The Facts about Alcohol and Tobacco.* New York: Macmillan, 1991.

———*The Facts about Crack and Cocaine.* New York: Macmillan, 1991.

Washton, Arnold M. and Donna Boundy., *Crack & Cocaine: What You Need to Know.* Hillside, NJ: Enslow Publishers, 1989.

Woititz, Janet G., *Adult Children of Alcoholics.* Deerfield Beach, FL: Health Communications, 1990.

———*Struggle for Intimacy.* Deerfield Beach, FL: Health Communications, 1985.

Index

About the Author

Glenn Cheney is a writer and a professor of writing at Fairfield University. Among the many topics he has written on are Mahatma Gandhi, television, the Amazon, Chernobyl, and Central America. His radio dramas, which teach English as a Second Language, are heard around the world on the Voice of America. His fiction, articles, poetry and radio dramas have won a number of awards. He lives in Connecticut with his wife and son.